Preface

In a companion booklet, **The Lutheran People**, we set forth a description of Lutheran Christians and pointed to their locales, their forms, their main teachings. That approach stimulated appetites for a somewhat more extensive and detailed set of responses to questions people have about Lutheranism. In this booklet we have tried to meet these tastes and requests in question-and-answer form. In preparation I read many books that brought to the surface the questions that we can conceive being asked most frequently by non-members and members alike. The generalizations about Lutheran opinion are based largely on scientific opinion samplings, but some are combined with this one historian-reporter's personal impressions, where clear data were absent.

The responses of a theological or doctrinal character derive from a lifetime of membership in the Lutheran Church, many years of theological education and continued reading in the Bible, and in both formal and unofficial Lutheran writing. I have not tried to speak in always safe, dull, middling and averaging kind of language. Instead, Pascal's dictum that one should encompass the extremes and then cover the ground between them has been my ideal, even where it has not been realized. This does not mean that every outrageous, maverick, idiosyncratic thing ever said by a Lutheran had to be taken into account, but I tried to be responsible to what broad and diverse sectors of Lutheranism have said or, more particularly, are saying.

Explicit quotations from the Bible and Lutheran confessions are rare. This is intentional. I have tried to conceive this as a restatement of the faith and practices in the language of today. Yet the classic and traditional biblical and confessional language stands behind these contemporary-sounding assertions. (Where someone disagrees, I would like to hear about it, for the sake of revision. Simply write me at the University of Chicago, Chicago, Illinois 60637.) The Lutheran teacher or pastor who might make use of these statements can easily correlate them with more familiar-sounding versions.

We conceive this booklet as a curiosity-arouser and, sometimes, satisfier; as a paperback for browsing; as an argument-starter or settler; as a base for more extensive and deeper probing; as a sequence that might begin to serve those contemplating joining the Lutheran Church; as a guide for those who have long been members and would like to brush up or to compare their understanding with that of one of their contemporaries. I picture it having use in adult confirmation classes, in campus ministry, or wherever groups of twentieth century adults would like to compare notes on the meaning of Lutheran witness in the Christian Church and the world. It may not fulfill all its intentions, but those intentions are, at least, quite clear.

I.
The Lutheran Core

Q: What is a Lutheran?

A: A Lutheran is a follower of Jesus Christ, a member of the Christian Church. He or she would be defined as an evangelical Christian. The term evangelical refers to a term Protestants like to use to point out that their faith centers in the good news of what God has done for people in Jesus Christ. Lutherans make up the largest and, among the larger churches, the oldest of the groups that are heirs to the Reformation of the Western church four or five centuries ago. There are about ten million Lutherans in the United States.

Q: Why do these Christians carry the name Lutheran?

A: Lutherans do not like it that their enemies gave them the name of Martin Luther (1483–1546), nor did Luther welcome such a designation for his fellowbelievers. But the name 'stuck,' so members of the Lutheran Church not only live with it, but enjoy remembering by means of it what God did through the sixteenth-century reformer. Sometimes Lutherans like to speak of theirs as the Church of the Augsburg Confession, but they do not stand much chance of getting others to call it that.

Q: Who was Martin Luther?

A: He was a fallible, energetic, robust, occasionally crude, never dull German monk who had tried to please God by living the disciplines of a monastery. But he experienced the wrath, not the love of God, for these efforts. A reading of the Bible, particularly the letters of Paul, led him to an experience of God's unmerited goodness. He became a preacher, reformer, church leader, author of scores of books, family man, and proclaimer of the fact that God forgives people out of love, through Jesus Christ.

Q: Does Lutheranism have distinctive teachings?

A: Members of the Lutheran Church will tell you that they simply teach what the Bible teaches, what true Christians of every age have believed. But then, they know that most other churches make similar claims. There must be some special reasons for their separate existence. Some of these reasons have to do with accidents of history and geography, with habit and custom. But Lutherans do think that at the heart of their belief is an accent that other Christians share, but not all stress so single-mindedly.

Q: What is the core or central accent?

A: A code word for the heart of Lutheran belief is the reality of "justification by grace through faith." People do not use the old sense of the word "justification" with much frequency any more. In this phrase "justification" means that God considers righteous, or makes just, people who make nothing of their own righteousness or justice. Instead, they accept God's gift of Himself, His love, His activity, in the death and rising again of His Son, Jesus Christ. Since no one deserves such love, people are saved by grace. Since they are grasped by it and do not reason or work their way into it, this grace is received 'by faith.'

Q: What does the central teaching have to do with the rest?

A: A Swedish churchman put it well when he said that all other Lutheran teachings are not strung together like pearls on a thread. Instead, they all radiate out from the glowing core of "justification by grace through faith." That God forgives sinners, gives them new life, lets them be His instruments in the world—all this throws a warm and bright light on everything else. God is then seen fundamentally as the agent of love, not of majesty or power or wrath, though Christians also experience these other dimensions of the reality of God.

Q: You make so much of Jesus Christ. What about him?

A: The members of this church share with most Christians everywhere the belief that Jesus of Nazareth, two thousand years ago, was uniquely the Son of God. In fact, they believe that he is this today, because he lives among them, even if not as a physical presence. Lutherans devote themselves to his teachings as they are recorded in the Gospels; they like to study his words and works and ways; to follow his example; to explore what his death on a cross of execution and his being raised to new life by his Father, mean for their own daily life. They welcome no confession that takes away from Jesus Christ anything of his fully divine or his fully human character.

Q: If you make so much of Jesus, what happens to God?

A: Lutherans believe in God and confess faith in the Trinity. "The Trinity" is not a biblical word, but the word which was coined by early Christians, is based on biblical realities. Through this formula believers try to hold in perfect unity three 'persons' of God and, for them, three ways of experiencing or knowing God. He shows himself to be their Father or creator; he comes in the form of the servant and risen Lord Jesus Christ; he is present as the Holy Spirit who shapes the church and makes it holy. Lutherans do not believe that they have any special angle of belief on this way of speaking of God.

II.
Creeds and Confessions

Q: Where does one find the Lutheran teachings set forth?

A: Basically, the core beliefs were stated in several documents of the sixteenth century, though hundreds of more recent books—including this small one—have restated the faith in the terms of later times. Before we referred to the Church of the Augsburg Confession. The Augsburg Confession of 1530, since it was the first formal statement of the Lutheran element in Germany, remains determinative. Martin Luther's little digest, **The Small Catechism**, is a more convenient and more widely known summary of the faith.

Q: What are Confessions and Catechisms?

A: You hear about both terms in today's Lutheranism, so it is a good idea to say more. A confession in this case does not mean to say that you have done something wrong, though confession **can** mean that. Think of it instead as a kind of long creed, a statement of beliefs, a spelling-out of teachings. A catechism is a special form of such a confession or creed; it is usually cast in questions and answers—much as this little book is. In short, you have in your hand a confession and a catechism, though it is informal and unofficial and includes information that is not confessional in character.

Q: What makes a Lutheran a good Lutheran?

A: From what has gone before it is clear that the good Lutheran is not the one who has kept the most mimemographed rules or regulations, or who has worked the hardest to impress God. In place of all that, the good Lutheran is one who is aware of his or her shortcomings, willingly relies on God's action, rejoices in experience of God's forgiving love, and makes faith active in love for serving other people. The good Lutheran will regularly be in range of the places where the good news of grace is heard, will be a baptized participant at the Lord's Supper, will take part in the shared life of Christians.

Q: Don't the confessions or creeds define Lutheranism?

A: Indeed they do, but they define in a special way. In effect they say, "This we believe!" and not "This you must believe!" It is true that some Lutherans use them to build fences, to rule heretics out and the orthodox in, to enforce loyalty. But such activity is doomed over the long pull of history. People who share the confession cannot keep from being loyal and expressive; people who do not cannot be forced to pretend or to conform. The church is healthiest when it causes people to study, inquire, persuade each other, teach, willingly confess, and happily live the reality of grace and faith in Jesus Christ.

III.
The Bible Interpreted

Q: Again and again you make much of the Bible. Why?

A: The Bible, sixty-six ancient short writings, make up the sacred scriptures of all Christians. (Think of the volume as a library of stapled-together pamphlets, written by many different people over many centuries of time.) The Bible includes the Hebrew Scriptures of God's ancient people, the Old Testament, and a much shorter collection of books that grew up among the earliest Christians. The Bible is the story of God's dramatic dealing with His people, of His acts of creating them, rescuing them when they fell, leading them through history, giving them laws and promises. It is a collection of narratives, letters, songs, and prophecies.

Q: How do Lutherans regard the Bible, the Scriptures?

A: Awesomely. They yield to no other Christians in their regard for its authority. They allow no teaching to bind believers' consciences unless somewhere the Scriptures clearly teach it. They call it the only source and the only norm for measuring Christian teaching. That does not mean that they all agree at all times with each other in interpreting. But they do agree that no teaching can be considered seriously in the church if the one who holds it cannot even make the claim that it comes from the Bible.

Q: What is the nature of this Biblical authority?

A: Lutherans believe that the Bible is divinely inspired, that in some special way God saw to it that the humans who wrote it, without stepping outside their own personality and style, imparted His own truth. They believe that it is 'infallible' and unerring in its setting forth of all that one needs to be made right with God; Scriptures will not mislead believers. Some Lutherans go a step further and speak of the Bible as being 'inerrant' in the sense that its details are unfailingly accurate even when they talk about matters of geography, history, or 'science.' Most Lutherans do not begin with such statements, however; they adhere to the Bible because it brings them Jesus Christ and speaks with authority to them in matters of faith and hope.

Q: Are there distinctive ways Lutherans have of interpreting the Bible?

A: If by this is meant a single approach to its study, no. Some Lutherans think of themselves as literalists. (Literalists do not put Lutherans in their camp, because Lutherans are rarely literalist about revelational-dream-visionary language, and they give disproportionate attention to some parts of Scripture). Others make use of modern literary and historical techniques for understanding the original context and meaning of biblical texts. All serious Lutherans are serious also about hearing the Bible speak to them, through whatever scholarly means. Distinctiveness lies in a principle that Lutherans see throughout Scripture: the proper distinction between Law and Gospel.

Q: What does this 'proper distinction' imply?

A: The language derives form Martin Luther, who thought all theology was to be measured by it. He saw one God in one Word speaking two kinds of languages to two situations. In Lutheran interpretation, the Law is constituted to effect human relations but never to make humans right with God. It is a power of God for establishing the state and human society, for care of the neighbor. But in that matter of one's being saved or justified, the law always and only serves to accuse and condemn the sinner. Then the Gospel comes in to play its part, not as a system of new rules and regulations but to issue in spontaneous loving discipleship after reception of the gift of unmerited grace or favor from God. Confusion of these two languages and intentions misleads people from the plot of the Bible and God's revealed will.

Q: Are there other Lutheran distinctives in interpretation?

A: Yes. Another approach to which they devote themselves (again without claiming that no other Christians share the view) separates the theology of glory from the theology of the cross. Martin Luther coined the phrases. The first, which Lutherans reject, pictures humans attaining comprehension of the divine by reasoning their way into the Godhead or by speculation and contemplation. (Philosophy is welcomed, but not seen as effecting knowledge of or union with God.) The second, the theology of the cross, is content with receiving God's revelation, pursuing His tracks in history, especially through the Scripture, the life of the Church, the cross of Christ. It has an historical, event-centered, personalistic tinge.

Q: Do Lutherans believe in 'the right of private judgment'?

A: Yes and no. No, if this means that the individual Christian separates from the context of the Church and does anything he or she wants with the Bible. The Lutheran catechisms make clear that one hears the word in the setting of the Christian community; the Holy Spirit brings me to the Church where I hear and interpret the Word. The answer would be yes, however, if it means that the phrase implies personal study, appropriation, and the following of conscience on the basis of what one hears and reads in the Scripture. The phrase could be used if it means that people must understand or must believe for themselves even as they must die for themselves; but it is not much used in Lutheran circles, because it is partial and misleading as an approach.

IV.
Faith, Reason, and Human Nature

Q: So much is made of 'faith' in God and so on. What about reason?

A: Belief in God and acceptance of biblical authority are not seen to do away with human reason. We bring this up because Luther at times said unflattering things about reason; once he called it 'the devil's damned whore.' Such language obviously invites misunderstanding. Since Luther carried on his reform from within a university and made so much of learning, it could not mean that he was against the reason of man, in most contexts. He was nervous about only one sphere: he was surrounded by people who thought they could come to know God and be right with Him on the basis of their intellect and reasoning power. No. That would take away God's gracious initiative and deprive believers of the assurance that God was making them whole.

Q: How is reason then to be used?

A: Lutherans believe that God is to be loved "with heart and soul and **mind**." Reason does not set itself above God or the scripture. But it is employed both to help people think about what has been revealed, to set teachings in clear order, and to relate what God reveals to all the other dimensions of life—including science, philosophy, history and the like. All that the human being is can be converted from selfish purpose to the service of God; this is true of body and reason alike.

Q: Is the old warfare between science and faith over?

A: Many kinds of warfares between many kinds of science and many kinds of faith are over. Lutherans never saw any of these spheres as unitary wholes, and they dissect each to learn their origins, definitions, goals. Some Lutherans still see problems with consistent evolutionary teaching, when it is designed to give an utterly naturalistic accounting of human origins and development; others see in some kinds of transformed evolutionary thinking an enhancement of the scope of God's various ways of creating and sustaining life. Psychological behaviorism and certain attitudes in the realm of physics or geology might present special problems of interpretation. But none of these rule out positive relations between science and faith.

Q: You have made nothing of the human spiritual side; does it not help make people right with God?

A: Lutherans make much of human spirituality, but they do not believe it makes one right with God. In fact, they believe that it can get one into all kinds of trouble. Precisely in one's life of piety and prayer, meditation and contemplation, the temptation comes to lead one to think that his or her efforts have pleased God. These temptations are less storng in one's daily practical work and pleasures. When God has reached a person with His grace, **then** the spiritual side of humans is transformed into something glorious.

Q: You seem to have a pretty low view of human nature. Right?

A: Right. And a pretty high one. Lutherans have a 'low' view of the natural human because they see human history blighted by selfishness, greed, ignorance, folly and sin. They know themselves. They believe what the Bible has said about man's plight. But they also turn these views of nature and sin around. When God's righteousness becomes theirs by grace through faith in Christ, they believe and say the most extravagant things about humans. Luther did not merely believe that a Christian could become 'as Christ'; he or she could be **a** Christ. God looks at the forgiven sinner as one who wears Christ's robes of righteousness, as one who is His instrument for His saving purposes in the world.

V.
Sacraments and Ordinances

Q: What brings about the change from the natural sinner to the remarkably 'just' one?

A: Baptism. Hearing and believing the Word of God, whether spoken and preached—and Lutherans make much of the 'living' Word—or as it is found in various forms in the Scriptures. Sharing in the Lord's Supper. These have often been called the 'means of grace,' the avenues for God's first or renewed entry into the lives of His people.

Q: What goes on in Baptism?

A: Baptism is an act shared with most other Christians. Lutheranism's distinctive views grow out of the 'glowing core' of forgiveness. They see Baptism as an act ordained by Christ, one which combines the use of water (any amount, any form of application) on people of any age or circumstances, with the word of God that promises grace and forgiveness. This act is received in faith. It 'drowns' the old and natural being, and a new being in Christ emerges. Because Lutherans read of whole households being baptized in New Testament times, and because faith is a gift and not an achievement, they baptize infants, surrounded as they are by the faith of the believing community. Lutherans do not rebaptize other Christians who have been baptized in the name of the Holy Trinity and with the use of water.

Q: And the proclaimed or read Word of God?

A: Were there not a Word of God, people could know nothing of what God is or does for them. The eternal silence would be broken only by human chatter or by serious efforts to reason about how the world is put together. When someone proclaims the Word of God, an ancient story of God's dealings is made alive and applied to new circumstances. It is thus a living Word, fired by the Holy Spirit, and not a mere reflection about a remote past. Now, this word is spoken by fallible human beings. But God uses them for His ends, and grace can be imparted even through bad grammar and squeaky voices or misspelled words. The preaching of the Word of God, then, is an event important for faith.

Q: The Lord's Supper—what about it?

A: The New Testament shows Jesus, the night before he died, eating a ceremonial meal with his disciples. After it, he took bread and wine and identified it with his body and blood, which he then shared with them. From their participation in the body and blood of Christ the early church passed on a sacred meal, done in remembrance of Christ, an act of thanksgiving (eucharist) and fellowship (communion). Lutherans believe that the chief gift of this meal is, once again, God's forgiveness and a new life for those who repentantly and in faith share the Lord's Supper. Some Lutherans, Luther among them, by the way, also call this meal 'the mass.'

Q: How do you connect bread and wine with Christ's body and blood?

A: Faithfully. That is, in faithfulness to Jesus' own words as recorded in the Gospel. And in faith, since Lutherans do not believe that human reason can fully grasp what God does and how He does it in the Lord's Supper. Lutherans have often been in dispute with other Christians or with each other over the 'precisely how' of this identification. From these battles they have learned that no one can do a very good job. So they resort to language like this: Jesus is really present in this meal. Negatively stated, they do not think that it is only a memorial, a rite, a symbol. Positively: they share God's promise of Christ's presence when they gather for it.

Q: How many sacraments do Lutherans observe?

A: Baptism and the Lord's Supper are the only two acts that qualify by Lutheran definition, which includes only sacred acts, instituted by Christ, ordained by God, promising grace, and combining natural elements with the divine word. But you will not get an argument from Lutherans as to how many sacraments there are, if sacraments are differently defined by others. The term sacrament itself is not biblical at all. Lutherans have other rites that some other Christians call sacraments—marriage, ordination of clergy, and the like—but they use different designations for these.

Q: How often do Lutherans share in the sacraments?

A: Once for Baptism, 'Oft,' or often, for the Lord's Supper or Eucharist. Early Christians probably had the sacred meal every 'Lord's Day' and millions of Lutherans still do. In some Lutheran cultures communion is observed only monthly or, more rarely, quarterly. This less frequent observance tended to occur where Lutherans were surrounded by non-Lutheran Christians who made less of Holy Communion. In the twentieth century weekly opportunities are coming to be more common again. There are no rules and regulations governing observance; the Church of the Augsburg Confession pictures sinners hungry for a meal expressive of forgiveness, lonely people seeking Christian communion—frequently.

Q: How does one go about taking part in the Lord's Supper?

A: First, the Christian heart is searched, so that one approaches the Lord's Table with a sense of repentance (a sorrow for sin, an eagerness to turn). After the celebrant has repeated the Gospel's words of Christ's institution, bread and wine are distributed to the people. In most cases the people come forward to the altar or table to receive these elements. They make their approach reverently but not somberly, since they are going to a banquet, a feast of new life.

Q: How do adults become members of the Lutheran Church?

A: By conviction. Lutherans do not want people to join them only as a result of mixed marriages or social convenience; as time passes, these affiliations would become meaningless or be seen as hypocritical. Convinced people who share their basic understanding of the Gospel make up the marrow of Lutheranism. This does not mean that the tests of church membership are assents to thousands of doctrinal propositions; very simple, uneducated people grasp this Gospel and are members. Those who share the convictions and the faith are received by confirmation (or baptism, if they have not been baptized), or, in many cases, by profession of faith if they have been members of churches whose confession does not differ vastly from Lutheranism's. (Confirmation is an ordinance, not a sacrament; a covenanting act, not one that imparts grace.)

VI.
Worship and Its Setting

Q: Describe the context of baptizing, preaching and communing.

A: These can go on in lonely places—like maternity wards in hospitals or in sick rooms or on desert islands. But the vast majority of these celebrations of the Word occur in divine service. Such services at churches may be very simple occasions filled with Scripture, prayer and praise. They may be more formal observances. Lutherans originally kept most of what they could from Western Catholic services of their time. Roman Catholics often find many parallels between their worship and Lutherans' for example.

Q: What are the rhythms of this main service?

A: In addition to the expected invocations, benedictions, hymns, scriptures, preached Word and prayers, there is a broadly-followed outline. Formerly Lutheran used Latin words such as "Introit" or "Gradual" to mark the elements of the service. Today the terms are simpler. After "Confession and Forgiveness" there is a hymn, a Kyrie ("Lord, Have Mercy," a Greek term surviving!), a Hymn of Praise, a Prayer of the Day, readings of Scriptures, and a homily or sermon. Then follow the Creed, the Prayers, the Offertory and Offering, and, when there is communion, as there usually is, a Great Thanksgiving before people commune. Ordinarily before everything else, there will be a short service or an exchange of public but ritualized confessions of sins and proclamations of forgiveness.

Q: Confession is public and formal. May it be private and personal?

A: By all means. Lutherans retain but do not require the act of private confession. They can confess to each other and forgive each other at any time. They can confess through ritual forms and hear a Word of forgiveness pronounced to a group. But especially when a heavy burden of sin weighs one down, he or she may wish to speak privately with a confessor—usually a pastor—who is to keep the seal of confessional confidentiality. Many Lutherans wish more of their fellow-members would take advantage of this more dramatic but not different-in-kind confessional act.

Q: A word about worship. What happens to first-timers?

A: Regular church-goers probably cannot picture why this question is asked, but it is important for one who has never attended a service in a strange tradition. What happens? Nothing embarrassing. The degree of friendliness in the greeting may vary, alas!, from unthinking neglect born of old habits to a slightly too gushy greeting at the door. But most Lutherans will simply and naturally be glad you are there and will provide an order of service and hymnals or service books for you to take part 'as the spirit moves.' You should get a friendly invitation to return, but no pressure. Non-Lutherans should speak to the pastor before they commune; Lutheran practice on 'open communion' varies dramatically from place to place.

Q: A few questions about specifics of worship. Why do I see some Lutherans making the sign of the cross?

A: Nothing magical. Luther urged them to begin their day that way as a reminder of the sign of the cross made on them at baptism. It is a mark of rededication to that cross. Some Lutheran service books recommend that people 'sign' when receiving Holy Communion, or at the last phrase of the Nicene Creed; some Lutherans make the sign whenever the Trinity is invoked. Two things to remember: you will never be embarrassed should you **not** make the sign of the cross; you will never be thought of as receiving merit badges of a special kind from God if you do. But you may find it a good external reminder of deeply spiritual needs and gifts.

Q: What about handshakes and the 'kiss of peace'?

A: Moderns had made worship into a rather severe and staid intellectual affair. Recently, they have been trying to transcend their 'uptightness' and recover biblical concepts of worship and of the body. There is no question but that biblical worship was full of bodily movement, physical greetings, motion, dancing, eating and drinking, conversing, and the like. One sign of this recovery, now widely practiced during the act of reconciliation at Communion services, involves a simple greeting and the words about Christ's peace being passed. Some people follow biblical precedent and extend a kiss. Because long in disuse, these practices cannot be recovered without a bit of shuffling and nervousness. Relax.

Q: Candles, images, icons, kneelers: what about extenal artifacts and Lutheran worship?

A: They mean whatever Lutherans choose to let them mean. None need be present for full and effective worship. All may serve as reminders—especially in this television age when we think visually—of things spiritual. A candle may thus represent God's spiritual presence (more likely than it would stand for the reserved host or retained consecrated bread, which it may have signified in Catholic churches). A cross, statue, or picture is an aid to meditation, an enhancement of beauty, never confused in Lutheran circles with any magical ideas that such an object then becomes especially holy or full of powers.

Q: And saints, what do Lutherans make of these?

A: They believe that all Christian sinners are, in Christ, saints and to be thought of as such. They also recognize special saintliness in certain men and women of history; they do not pray to these, but they revere and remember them and regard them as examples. By accidents of history a few St. Martins and St. Lawrences and Saint Barbaras made their way into the names of a handful of American Lutheran congregations. But the only saints' days regularly observed by Lutherans are those of some biblical saints, including chiefly Jesus' original disciples.

Q: What festivals do Lutherans observe?

A: They kept the whole round of church-year events practiced and observed by medieval Catholicism, rejecting those only that they believed to be unevangelical (e.g., if they seemed to impart magical significance to the bread of the Lord's Supper). By the whole round, I mean the cycle that begins with Advent, anticipating Christ's nativity at Christ-mass; then the Sundays of his Epiphany, pre-Lent, Lent, Holy Week climaxed in Easter, Pentecost or Whitsunday fifty days later, and then a sequence of Sundays through summer into autumn, after Pentecost or Trinity Sunday. Regular Scripture readings are set aside for these, so that every year a congregation can rehearse the rhythms of the events through which God acted toward His people.

Q: Are there any approved clerical vestments for worship?

A: No. In the sixteenth century the academic gown was adopted for preaching services, and it survives here and there. In the twentieth century there is considerable recovery of the historic eucharistic vestments, topped by a chasuble, as worn by Roman Catholic priests at formal services. Somewhere along the way, largely by accident or under subtle Episcopal cultural influences, the majority of American Lutheran ministers adopted a kind of informal uniform: a white alb, over which falls a colored stole to match the colors of the church year. During communion some wear a chasuble, a kind of cape, usually with symbols of communion on it. Ministers may or may not choose to wear a clerical collar 'off the premises.' No big deal.

Q: Is any architectural style peculiarly Lutheran?

A: No. Lutherans simply took over some Catholic churches of Europe and 'cleaned them out' to some extent. Through the centuries, local and ephemeral architectural styles dominated more than did any attempt at explicit Lutheran expression. In the twentieth century many have noticed the Lutheran predisposition toward experimental expressions; they have been in the advance guard of architectural renewal. Most Lutheran churches accent pulpit and altar; the font should be prominent. From there on, almost any arrangement is workable. Most churches have fixed pews; this is unfortunate, because it inhibits movement and activity and causes most people to think of worship posture as looking at the back of one other Christian's head. But even this situation is improving.

Q: You seem pleased with the architecture, at least in some cases. Any other esthetic glories?

A: Oh, yes, The music. Hymnody is rich in Lutheran traditions, and Lutherans like to sing. When ministers get together for conferences, they beller the chorales, the old now-translated German and sometimes Scandinavian hymns. These are God-centered, not subjective (full of "I, I, I"), and stately; they were the base for many elaborations of genius by people like J. S. Bach. And Lutherans do fairly well with contemporary experimental music. They also have often imported a good amount of the intervening Victorian, man-centered, banal hymnody along the way. More's the pity. But you cannot have everything. And some of the imports have increased Lutheranism's appeal and informed its sense of involvement with other Christians.

Q: Much is made today of spiritual life; do Lutherans practice techniques of spirituality?

A: They pray—at table, in private, together in congregations. They have always encouraged meditation, and are recovering the art. They have not uniformly nurtured mysticism; if mysticism implies a union achieved with God on His level, this contradicts Lutheran belief that God condescends on His initiative to our own. If it means being receptive to that condescension and identification in Christ, Lutherans encourage 'mystical awareness.' They simply do not believe that by these techniques and approaches, healthy as they may be, people should conceive of themselves as having attained or merited God's grace and favor.

Q: One recovery of our day is in pentecostal tongue-speaking. Is there a Lutheran position on it?

A: Yes, an ambiguous one. Lutherans do not deny that early Christians experienced tongue-speaking as a gift of the Holy Spirit and they do not see the promise of its possibility cut off in subsequent history. There are Lutheran charismatics and pentecostalists who prophecy, interpret, heal, and speak in unintelligible language. Their fellow Lutherans often admire certain aspects of their spirituality. They regard these gifts as lowest in biblical ranking, however, and therefore do not welcome advertisements for these as granting superior status to Christians in God's or men's sight. They fear the divisiveness pentecostalists often bring; they are trying to understand what is going on; they cannot accept concepts of a 'second baptism' as rendering baptism itself incomplete.

VII.
The Faiths of Other People

Q: How do Lutherans relate to other churches?

A: On the basis of the Gospel. They believe that for the true unity of the Church it is enough to agree on the Good News of God and the sacraments. Rites, ceremonies, ways of governing the church are secondary. So, ever since the Augsburg Confession of 1530, they have thought of themselves as being 'ecumenical.' They believe that Christ's Church is always in the process of becoming aware of its oneness, and that no Christian should fail to recognize this. Such a realization does not mean, of course, that they believe that a growing Christian unity should come at the expense of local color, distinctive cultural traditions, and variety of expressions.

Q: If Lutherans are for unity, why are they divided?

A: They are divided among themselves—you noticed that?—chiefly over inherited cultural habits; they arrived in America in different waves of immigration, from different European nations, and made different kinds of adjustments to the American scene. Today they have boiled down most of their denominations to three or four large groups, and these agree on most things most of the time. But if they do spot minor theological differences, they tend to make a major case of them, and work them out before uniting. The Church lives between the poles of contending for truth and contending for unity. Lutherans, for better or for worse, have sometimes done less for unity than for the zeal for truth.

Q: Are you saying, then, that Lutherans have a bad record ecumenically?

A: On a world-wide scale, not at all. From the Reformation until early in the twentieth century they often were part of the timid steps being made toward unity. In the twentieth century pioneers like Nathan Soderblom of Sweden helped form the great ecumenical conferences and councils, and some American Lutherans played their part. With the exception of one synod or two, Lutherans are characteristically participants in unitive activities and councils, from local through state to national and world levels. And even the conservatives who stood off from the larger ecumenical movement have often learned to 'team up' with Reformed conservative evangelicals for many kinds of activities. But they are never casual or sentimental about such efforts.

Q: How do Lutherans relate to Eastern Orthodox or Roman Catholics?

A: Because of geographical remoteness, they have had little live experience of Orthodoxy, but a student of both will find many points of overlappage—particularly in their celebration of the Resurrection. So far as western Catholicism is concerned, relations vary dramatically from generation to generation. In our century Lutherans and Catholics are very close on many issues that once separated them —particularly since the open conversations following Vatican II (1962-1965). They also remember what they regard as the original reason for separation—a dispute about grace and faith—and recall many periods of hostility, but they also find much to admire in Catholicism.

Q: What does Lutheranism admire about Catholicism?

A: Through all the centuries, it has appreciated Catholicism's clear Trinitarian faith—when many Protestants wavered in that faith. Even when it disagreed about how grace in Christ reaches humans, the Lutheran Church admired Catholicism for keeping Christ central. While Lutherans did not appreciate the idea of seeing Mary as a Co-Redemptrix, they valued Catholicism's view of Mary as 'Mother of God.' The Church of the Augsburg Confession kept what it could of Catholic liturgy, piety, hymnody, devotional expression, and the like. So members of the two churches never felt themselves to be wholly on 'foreign soil' when they were in contact with the other. Lutherans also admired Catholics' dedication. But only after about 1965 could these often hidden bonds come to light.

Q: Is Lutheranism Protestant or Catholic?

A: Yes. It is Protestant **or** Catholic, depending upon which side of the poles of its existence one is appraising. Lutherans are Protestants as evangelicals who centered on grace and faith, and as protestors against papal authority in matters of faith and morals. But they are Catholic in their desire to be seen in continuity with the Church of all ages; their intention to be universal; their goal of having faith reach into the depths of being and reality (for 'catholic' means all of that). For a long time many Lutherans were nervous about the term 'catholic,' even in their creeds, because many identified that term with Roman Catholicism. Today that nervousness is passing.

Q: What about Lutherans and Jews?

A: A touchy subject. Lutherans inherited many Western Christian attitudes toward Jews, and helped keep them in ghettos, making no effort to understand them. Luther began on good terms with Jews; when they failed to convert he turned vehemently against them and said things which later Lutherans have to regret and just as vehemently repudiate. In modern time, Lutherans have proven to be no more anti-Semitic in practice than their other Christian neighbors, but sometimes their educational literature perpetuated theological stereotypes that laid special guilt upon Jews. (When this was pointed out several years ago, they rethought the effects of such habitual teaching and made appropriate changes.)

Q: Did Lutherans have a role in the holocaust?

A: The holocaust, in which six million Jews were murdered in the Nazi era, occurred in part on traditionally Lutheran soil (of Eastern Germany). Historians now remind us that the attempt to 'do in' all Jews did not come in past 'Christian centuries,' when it would have been easy, but in a secular century. But many Christians, including many Lutherans, went along with their nation's over-all program, in the case of Nazism. The records do show that the Jewish extermination policies were in the hands of secular or pagan repudiators of the faith. And many Lutherans witnessed for and died for their faith over against the perpetrators of Nazi anti-Jewish policy. But Lutherans became especially aware of the need to repent and change Christian-Jewish relations.

Q: Is there a happier side to Lutheranism's understanding of Jews and Judaism?

A: Indeed, yes. Along with repentance and mind-changing, practical good relations, and formal conferences or study projects to improve the situation, much more can be said. Through all the centuries the Lutherans devoted themselves highly to the Hebrew Scriptures or the Old Testament. Thus, they regarded Jews as 'people of the promise.' They may have considered them spiritually 'half-finished products,' participants in only the first act of a two-act drama. But the Jews **were** part of the drama. Lutheran biblical students have taught their fellow Christians to reread Romans 9-11, to see that the covenant between God and Jews has not been broken and that Christians are a branch grafted on to the tree of God's ancient people.

Q: What about other religions?

A: The issue did not come up much until the nineteenth century, when Euro-Americans came into contact with other faiths (Hinduism, Buddhism, Islam, and the like). Most of the early reactions to these faiths were distorted, born of ignorance and lack of empathy, exaggerated by missionaries. In the course of time Lutherans have come to a generally more positive understanding of what the cultures, traditions, and faiths of other peoples have meant in their lives. They portray them less negatively and are less ready simply to try to see them denigrated or annihilated than they would have been a century ago.

Q: Does such a changed attitude make universalists out of Lutherans?

A: No. Universalism can be defined as a belief that God's love reaches out through all the faiths and non-faiths, so that whatever one believes, in the end he or she will be 'saved.' Lutherans believe the scriptural word that there is no other name by which people will be saved than by the name Jesus Christ. So they try to share that name. But they also know that, after they have done all they can in that name, God's purposes are not thereby exhausted; He may have unannounced plans congruent with His love, for dealing with those who never comprehended explicit faith in Christ. If so, any such 'saving' would still go on in the name of Jesus Christ.

VIII.
Missions and Peoplehood

Q: That means, then, that Lutherans have been missionary people?

A: Yes. Have been and are. They pioneered in Protestant missions in the eighteenth century, beginning in India. For over a century they have participated in the modern missionary movements, out of continental and American bases, 'into all the world.' They believe that all people should have the opportunity to hear of Christ; they believe that the works of love should go with the proclamation. So they have built schools and hospitals. Like most other Christians, they have not lived up to all their intentions for the world-wide mission, but they have always believed in it and have always had intentions. They see what Christ has done for them and cannot picture that it would not similarly save and enhance the existences of others.

Q: Closer to home, are they evangelistic?

A: If by that is meant, do they employ the techniques of revivalism and evangelism, the answer has been generally no. Recently this situation has changed and many Lutherans have been influenced by non-Lutheran styles. But for the most part they have not relied on mass evangelism, or on special emotional circumstances and forms of preaching designed for instantaneous conversion. They have not generally shared revivalists' views of the potency of human will in the desire for conversion, and have shunned attempts at psychological manipulation of peo-

Q: Well, then, they don't sound very evangelistic.

A: Not on conventional terms. But on their own terms, they are. They believe that it is inevitably of the character of the Church of Jesus Christ to grow, for his reconciling circle to expand. But they also believe that special means must be undertaken for that growth. Every Lutheran sermon is to include an explicit statement of the Gospel, presented so winningly that the previously unreached cannot miss the appeal. Lutherans have many programs and committees for going out, especially through local congregations, to the unchurched in their communities. They send missionaries into areas little touched as yet by Lutherans in America. But they most of all try to train all their members to witness and to live the Christian way among their neighbors, and thus to attract others.

Q: You mention areas where there are few Lutherans. Do Lutherans proselytize?

A: No. They never seek to win people who are already members of Christian churches, where these people are reached by the Gospel—even if Lutherans do not agree with all that goes on in such churches. They do instinctively and often explicitly believe in a kind of 'division of labor,' wherein other Christians will take on some tasks that Lutherans then will not touch. But with the flow of population in mind and with the desire that the Lutheran option be available, they are trying to be a presence in new suburbs, in once-deserted inner cities, and in parts of the country where they have been under-represented.

Q: Isn't a ten-million member church pretty national?

A: Of course it is, in a 'thin-spread' way. But American Christians are still amazingly regionalized on denominational lines. Utah is Mormon. All but three tips of the South finds Baptist majorities. The mid-South and lower North is Methodist. The coasts, the Great Lakes, the three southeran tips in Texas, Louisiana, and Florida, are chiefly Catholic. The Lutheran 'strongholds' are the middle West and upper Midwest, leading out to the far Northwest, with strong representations in a belt that goes from New Jersey and the Carolinas through Pennsylvania and Ohio. New England and the South find the smallest Lutheran proportions.

Q: Why this kind of geographical distribution?

A: The answer has to do largely with times of Lutherans' arrivals in America. They were not welcomed in Congregational New England, so they first settled in the middle colonies of New Jersey, New York, and especially Pennsylvania or in the upper South, in North Carolina and Virginia. In the nineteenth century they spilled West from there. But this continental minority, still quite small in the 1830s, came to be swelled by hundreds of thousands of new German and Scandinavian immigrants thereafter; at that time the midwest and the upper midwest were opening up for immigration, and they filled up this new space.

Q: Is Lutheranism, then, an ethnic family?

A: Like most other denominations, it is true that Lutheranism does show strong reminiscences of its European past. Not a single, white American church body has seen a fundamental shift in European ethnic make-up. That is, no groups that came from southern Europe have turned Protestant (Italians, Spaniards, etc.) in America, nor have northern Protestant peoples turned Catholic. Congregationalists and Presbyterians derive largely from the British Isles, as do the Episcopalians. And Lutherans are largely of Scandinavian and German background. Through evangelism, inter-marriage, suburban expansion, and accidental effects of mobility, there is far more ethnic variety in Lutheranism than before, but Lutherans have a long way to go to be truly represented among all the American peoples.

Q: What about minority peoples?

A: Because of the geographical picture just spelled out, the reader can surmise that Lutherans are under-represented among blacks. A moment ago we said that there have been few intra-European ethnic shifts among denominations. But Baptists and Methodists in the south, where blacks were concentrated, were remarkably successful at spreading among them. Largely under auspices of Negro leadership, these denominations came to number millions of blacks, while Lutheranism in the north and midwest had neither the contacts, the vision, the zeal, or the genre of church life to attract many blacks. For some years strenuous efforts have been made, but until now the story has been 'too little and too late.' Yet thousands and thousands of blacks are making their presence felt in Lutheran circles.

Q: Blacks are not the only minority. What about others?

A: So far: at least as bleak. Lutherans share other European-Americans' terrible record toward the American Indian, so far as being a presence among them, understanding them, or serving them is concerned. A third large minority, of Spanish background, comes largely from Catholic countries, and there are yet few Lutherans among them. The picture is becoming clear. Churches have tended to follow ethnic lines, realized this rather late, have been trying to change it, notice that change is glacial, are stepping up efforts. This must be said: on principle and, one hopes increasingly in practice, all people of all races and peoples are supposed to feel welcome by Lutherans, whose Gospel is for all people, even when they themselves do not know fully how to realize that.

IX.
A Kind of Exclusivism?

Q: I have heard that not all Lutherans approve all clubs and fraternal organizations. What about that?

A: In general, Lutherans do not try to keep their people captive of their own interest groups and organizations. They do not measure the depth of Christian devotions by counting kilowatt hours of electricity spent for lighting up their churches every night to keep their people together. They believe in having Christ's people go out and serve the world through witness and presence in countless organizations, movements, and interest groups. Once upon a time, as struggling ethnic and religious groups in an environment they regarded to be non-comprehending and hostile, there may have been more 'xenophobia,' fear of strangers, or more ethno-centrism, an attempt to keep people together. Most of that has changed.

Q: Most, but not all. Are there 'off-limit' organizations?

A: All Lutherans would say that there are off-limit organizations for Christians. To take two extreme examples: the Ku Klux Klan and the American Nazi Party. The only controversial residual issue about organizations on which there is some dispute among Lutherans ('check your local outlet for details') has to do with some fraternal orders on the lines of Freemasonry. Some suspicion was once born of Masonry's earlier European anticlericalism and (sometimes) anti-Christianity. But in America Masonry provides a milder and, of course, 'pro-God' option. But many Lutherans see such fraternal orders offering a way of salvation that bypasses salvation in Jesus Christ, and thus shun these.

Q: Are no Lutherans, then, members of these orders?

A: As with most churches, practices on matters of this sort vary widely and can be said to run the whole spectrum of alternatives. In some regions and branches of American Lutheranism, laity and clergy alike are also members of secret societies, in open good standing in both. In others, there is a clear line drawn between the two. In most situations, there is a 'case by case' approach. What is involved in membership of a secret society? Does the member in any way compromise distinctive faith in Christ? Is his or her participation chiefly for social purposes or good works? If a Lutheran congregation clearly found something incompatible between such a society and the Gospel, it would be hard to picture this group encouraging membership. This whole matter is less controversial than it was some years ago.

Q: The comments on world religion and secret societies suggest that Lutherans make much of 'truth.' Right?

A: Yes. Both their churches' virtues and vices are largely born of their wrestling with this issue. Vices: they sometimes have tended toward spiritual arrogance, cocksureness, standoffishness, erring on the side of literal definitions. The virtues: they want to be in the world as witnesses that God's truth matters, that faith can be dissipated and dissolved or denied by the admixture of too much casualness and, eventually, error. They make more than some churches do of the content of faith ('believing **that**' is mixed in with 'believing **in**'), and cherish the quest for or statement of truth, even at the risk of occasionally sounding or being attitudinally wrong. Still, they agree with the Bible: love is prior to the claims men make for the truth they hold.

X.
Practical Churchmanship

Q: How do Lutherans support their churches?

A: In Europe, they were largely established and thus somehow state- and tax-supported. In America they have been unanimous and enthusiastic participants in the voluntary system, believing that it best permits the love-ethic and idea of sacrificial service of the New Testament to stand out. Lutherans have not been wealthy people. Their churches are rarely if ever in any way endowed. They live off the support of generous people who weekly make provision for giving of their resources. They call such an approach 'stewardship.'

Q: How do they understand stewardship?

A: The minister on Stewardship Sunday mentions time, talent, and treasures. The congregation, especially the semi-cynical, probably translates that: treasures. Money. The minister or steward definitely does begin with time; the Christian who not only apportions specific parts of the week for service of God will also yield Him all the week, and will thus see treasures and talents in a new light. The one who turns his or her talents over to God will have no difficulty knowing God as the source of all treasures. But in a money-society, one that does not trade on oats, or kindling, or other barter, gifts of money are crucial if the work of the Church locally and abroad is to go on.

Q: What is expected?

A: Lutherans often like to propagate the biblical ideal of the tithe, one-tenth of income, and many leaders live up to it, though as a denomination Lutherans do less well on this front than Latter-Day Saints, Nazarenes, and the like. Many recognize that the biblical tithe included much welfare activity that taxes today cover. Lutherans would be delighted if a tithe on 'net income after taxes' would be universalized—and they even settle for less. What matters is that the gift come from the first, not the last of the income; that it be regularly provided for; that its purpose and motives be clearly understood; that it come forth cheerfully from people. Many congregations rely on pledged giving, but treat pledges and gifts confidentially.

Q: Where does the money go?

A: Inevitably, most money given for Christ goes to and is spent through local churches, for their programs, their leaders' salaries, their upkeep, their buildings. Most congregations wish (they say) that more could be sent and spent for missions, evangelism, publishing, medical care, welfare, and the like. Most congregations make commitments beyond their own needs to national Lutheran synods or organizations and outlets and then support numerous other options (e.g., Bible societies, colleges and seminaries, and the like) of their choice. With the exception of some subsidized new missions, most local congregations 'own'—that is, they are stewards in that time and place of—their own church building.

XI.
Leadership

Q: Where do these ministers and leaders come from?

A: Lutherans believe that their pastors (the preferred term, meaning 'shepherd' or one who takes care of people) should be 'properly called.' That has normally implied formal theological training, usually in church-approved seminaries. There are often other routes for ministers who come from other denominations or people of 'late vocation' who are trained privately or who essentially train themselves. But these avenues are rare. Ordinarily a congregation can have confidence that a Lutheran minister will have received intensive training and will have made careful studies of the Bible, Christian history, theology, Lutheran teaching, and the like.

Q: How do pastors come and go?

A: Especially with young congregations or starting-out ministers, a board or collection of leaders of a Lutheran denomination will 'send' them. In most other cases, however, they are 'called' by local congregations. These calls are understood to be for life—which has come to mean until retirement age—but in the American pattern of mobility it is probable that ministers are called and move elsewhere about as often as other people move, every five years or so. Where professional leaders and congregations do not mesh or creatively interact, the counsel of ecclesiastical superiors is often called upon to try to arrange a move for a pastor or other leader. Remarkably, in this fallible set-up, the chemistry seems to work right more often than not, and there are countless beautiful examples of pastors and people happily linked.

Q: Are ministers ordained?

A: Yes. Lutherans make much of ordination, though they have not clearly defined it. Since—recall the definition of sacraments?—they do not see ordination as employing visible means or imparting a different special grace, they do not think of it as a sacrament. Instead it is a profound spiritual act, in which a pastor takes on willingly and under oath the burden, responsibility, and joy of living into and trying to live up to the teachings, mandates, and promises of God for the Church of Jesus Christ. In ordination, the minister pledges to teach in congruence with the Scriptures as the only source and norm of teaching and with the Lutheran confessions as a faithful exposition of that teaching. He or she is also to live a godly life.

Q: He or she? Women ministers?

A: Through most Lutheran history, no. In recent European history, yes. In most recent American history, the beginnings of a yes. Two large Lutheran groups in America now ordain women to full ministry of word and sacraments. The idea is not controversial in those churches, but a full realization of the ideal comes slowly, as practices and mentalities change gradually. The move toward women ministers parallels the general contemporary rise in the consciousness of women's roles in world and church, and is seen by advocates as a working out of the logic of Paul's proclamation that in Jesus Christ there is no longer 'male nor female' but all are one in Christ.

Q: Does not Paul forbid women's formal ministry?

A: Sometimes, yes. Curiously, in the same chapter of I Corinthians (11) wherein he tells women not to prophesy he also tells them to wear head-coverings when they **do** prophesy! Clearly, we are seeing in two or three chapters of the New Testament, a working out of attitudes toward ministry and gender colored and conditioned by the culture of the time. For many Lutherans these chapters are seen as clear divine prohibitions, to stand for all ages. For the others, now in the majority, they are seen as something appropriate for their day, but time-bound and thus no longer binding. They point to the very many instances in Old and New Testaments where women did preach publicly, pray, prophesy, and in other ways act as ministers.

Q: The matter is not settled, then?

A: In a way it is settled in all but a few large Lutheran bodies in Europe and America; in the Evangelical Lutheran Church in America, for instance, hundreds of women were ordained during the past generation and have taken their place in ministry. The issue is complicated in some Lutheran bodies because of their understandings of both gender and the meanings of ordination.

Q: Well, then, what is a layman to Lutherans?

A: First of all, it is lay person, not layman. Second, we are not sure. From one point of view, all Christians are lay (**laos**, the root word, refers simply to the people of God) and they are all in ministry. Lutheranism is clear: before God, laity and professional set-aside clergy are equal. Their functions overlap. Lay persons baptize in emergency. They may and very frequently do at least assist at the Lord's Supper and could administer it effectively without a cleric at hand. A key concept in Lutheranism has to do with things being done 'in good order,' so the churches are careful not to blur wholly the line between formally ordained professional ministers and other Christians. (Laymen and laywomen on occasion also preach; they all are to absolve or forgive the penitent, as well.)

Q: Who are these other leaders about whom you have spoken?

A: Lutherans make much of teaching and teachers, from directors of Christian education, through parochial school teachers (as some American Lutheran groups have parish day schools) to college and seminary professors. They are usually called and set aside, often ordained for the ministry of teaching. Chaplains abound, in institutions and in the military. In nineteenth century Europe and in today's Europe and America there are orders of deaconesses, who engage in many set-aside and formally established ministries. Missionaries, nurses, administrators, staff workers, denominational executives—all these are part of today's complex church life.

Q: What about monks and nuns?

A: Because of Lutheranism's revolt against much that monasticism represented, the monastic ideal pretty well died out. Only in our times has there been the hint of a beginning of a restoration. America has only a couple of Lutheran monks, and no nuns. Germany and Scandinavia sew fewer reestablishments of Protestant or at least non-Roman monasticism than did nineteenth century England's Anglicanism or today's French formed establishment, as at Taize. But the repudiation was only in practice; in theory Lutheranism certainly does not rule out the values of celibacy, poverty, and obedience as avowed ideals for special Christian vocations.

XII.
Church Government

Q: How is Lutheran church government organized?

A: Lutheranism insists on no single polity. The Lutheran Church of Sweden believes that bishops in apostolic (unbroken) succession are essential for the life of the Church. In Denmark, Norway, Finland, and Germany the Lutherans have bishops as an important but not essential feature. In America the synods and their districts have presidents who act out the role of bishops, but in most groups are not called bishops. In practice, most Lutheran churches in America are fundamentally congregational, but they are linked in something like presbyteries and in synods (where people 'walk together'). Lutheranism, then is episcopopresbygational in its organization.

Q: What powers do congregations have?

A: They have taken on quite democratic models. Temporary exceptions may be made for heavily subsidized congregations that in effect remain a branch or arm of a missionary agency. But most other congregations determine most features of their own life: they call pastors, they receive and dismiss and excommunicate members, choose to build or not to build, to support or not to support, to invest or not to invest, and the like. In matters of spiritual life and confession they all, of course, choose to express themselves through the Scriptures, the ancient ecumenical creeds, and the Lutheran confessions of the nineteenth century. One or two groups have recently tried to impose or make binding their own synodical statements, but this is not a characteristic Lutheran activity, nor is the matter settled.

Q: What powers do extra-congregational agencies then have?

A: They have voluntary powers, powers of persuasion, powers granted them by congregations—at least in the pattern of American Lutheranism. They symbolize access to the whole Lutheran fellowship and Christian body. They coordinate activities that local churches cannot undertake alone. They often make provision for education of leaders, or publishing, or missionary life. They provide opportunities for lay and clerical delegates of congregations across the nation to come together for planning, study, the making of statements and pronouncements, the attempt to keep creedal and confessional statements fresh in the minds of Lutheran church people. But they do not dominate; in theory and sometimes in practice Lutheran congregations are independent of synods and yet are not considered heretical.

Q: We've mentioned heresy and excommunication a couple of times. What does Lutheranism have to do with these?

A: Lutheranism very definitely has a concept of heresy, which is not a minor unintentional deviation from something Lutherans believe to be true, but a clear or often intentional assault on or deviation from the Gospel and all that it implies. In most of its history, Lutheranism has had little trouble with heresy, because people have not wanted to be part of a church whose basic confession they do not share. Excommunication more frequently has to do with moral than with cognitive ('believe that,' or knowledge) questions.

Q: What is involved, then, in excommunication?

A: It is today a fairly rare act, undertaken by local congregations following procedures outlined in Matthew 18. Suppose a person lives in open sin, scandalizing the church, confusing the community. His fault is told him privately; if there is no repentance, some elders are brought on the scene; eventually, if there is no change, the unrepentant one is barred from the Holy Communion (hence, 'excommunicated'). He or she may attend church, should hear the preaching, is not to be socially shunned, since the act is designed to point to the gravity of the offense and to lead toward a changed way of life and to reaffirmation. Needless to say, formal excommunication routes are sometimes traumatic and not always effective. Nor is God bound to ratify the acts that sometimes mistaken and always fallible humans undertake.

XIII. Moral Questions and the Span of Life

Q: I have some questions about the cycle of life. Let's begin with birth control. What do Lutherans teach?

A: A century ago when modern birth control devices were being publicized, Lutherans joined most Protestants in being negative. They believe in families, and did not want people shirking responsibilities. They did not understand the full implications of family planning. Today in a crowded world, they read the Bible and see it asking people to be stewards of the earth. Too rapid population growth ends such stewardship. So they believe in family planning. The vast majority of the world's Lutherans favor birth control methods in the context of stewardship, responsibility, and marital love.

Q: What about abortion?

A: Abortion is a much more difficult and perplexing matter. Most Lutherans advocate therapeutic abortion, as when a mother's life might be in danger. Most oppose what many would call 'casual abortion' based on the belief that "a woman's body is her own, to do with what she wants." So abortion-on-demand does not get much of a ready hearing in Lutheran circles. Lutherans believe that 'we are members one of another,' that more people than just a pregnant woman are involved in pregnancies and should be consulted in decisions about possible termination of these. Some Lutherans are active in Right to Life agencies, a few in 'abortion on demand' movements, but most are 'in between.'

Q: What does 'in between' mean? What good does that do anyone?

A: For those Lutherans who do not simply equate abortion with murder, as if fetal life were not merely potential personal life but also developed personalhood, there are numerous options. They would argue that because Lutherans do not baptize the fetus, they must regard it differently than they do one-minute-old babies who may be dying. They want to be sure that anti-abortion forces regard all life as precious—for example in relation to capital punishment and war. They would say that the fetus has rights, but the fetus alone does not have all the rights. They would not excommunicate Lutherans who vote for 'abortion reform' laws in legislatures and the like.

Q: Moving on in the cycle: what about premarital sex?

A: The sexual act in its most profound and intimate form implies for Lutherans a sharing inside a life-long covenanted context of the form that marriage provides. In times past some conservative Lutherans believed that betrothal amounted to marriage, and were not against premarital acts between engaged couples; opinion polls reflect that attitude surviving here and there. But engagement has become more casual, more easily broken in contemporary society, so even in that setting extramarital intercourse is frowned upon.

Q: What are Lutheran views of marriage and marital sexuality?

A: Lutherans are quite serious about the biblical words that two in marriage become 'one flesh,' and are set apart only for each other. Marriage for them is a civil act and not a sacrament, but should be solemnized with pledges before the Lord's altar. They believe that expressions of sexuality within marriage can be highly diverse, so long as both parties find them congenial. There have been puritan moments in Lutheran history, but in general a hearty and robust attitude toward bodily expression in marriage prevails.

Q: Extramarital sexual intercourse—that's out?

A: Yes, because it is clearly and explicitly biblically 'out.' Casual moderns often fail to comprehend how deep and meaningful the biblical concept of 'one flesh' can be, how rich the commitment, how important the covenants and pledges made in marital vows. Two people 'count on each other' and become 'heirs together of the grace of life.' Extramarital intercourse jeopardizes and indeed violates the relation. On the other hand, Lutherans are trained to be acceptant of those who turn from their way after lapses, and do not want to make extramarital sexual intercourse the 'only sin in the book' just because it inspires such nervousness, gossip, and sense of superiority among those who do not fall.

Q: And divorce?

A: The Lutheran Church is steadfastly opposed to divorce—even if one out of three or four marriages in our society end in divorce. Their grasp of biblical understandings, their sense of pledges and vows, their concept of the union of two in 'one flesh' makes divorce on one level inconceivable. Yet Lutheran churches have many divorced and (by Lutheran clergy) remarried members. How can this be? Lutherans regard the brokenness and ambiguity of life not with sentimentality or a casual spirit but with empathy and a forgiving spirit. People who have marital problems are asked to take them up with a pastor or other experienced spiritual marital counselor; there **are** circumstances short of adultery where divorce is 'the only way.' But such counsel is not lightly given.

Q: What about euthanasia at the end of life?

A: Modern medicine presents new problems about the termination of life. Many people lead apparently meaningless and often excruciatingly painful existences 'as vegetables' long after there is any medical hope of any sort—thanks to improvements in medicines and devices that artificially prolong life. In face of this many thoughtful people, Lutherans among them, are agonizing over the question as to whether there can be circumstances in which such victims may be 'permitted to die.' There is no standard Lutheran resolution of this question, one that will be intensely debated in the years ahead. Lutherans do want to bring their high regard for the meaning of life to such debates.

Q: Now we are on subjects of personal morality. What about dancing?

A: That question comes up because many Lutherans in the not too distant past were quite critical of social dancing. Why they chose this practice for special opposition is not clear, because they were not notably puritan on many subjects. Some feared its sexual implications; others did not like the settings or contexts where it occurred; there may well have been hidden fears that Lutherans would meet and marry non-Lutherans at such gatherings (as, indeed, they sometimes did). Polls in our time show that few clergy and even fewer lay people are opposed to social dancing 'in moderation' today.

Q: What about gambling?

A: Lutheranism is not essentially a 'rules and regulations' church, so few have spelled out specific prohibitions against, say, gambling. Some Lutherans may gamble. But you will also find the practice frowned upon. It is regarded as part of a way of life that often fails to take account of 'stewardship,' of how God places possessions in human trust. It can consume peoples' lives, waste resources, contribute to crime, and the like. Still, despite the frowns, most Lutherans find more important ethical problems to deal with than gambling.

Q: Smoking and drinking?

A: Once upon a time many Lutheran ministers smoked, and made little point of it. As the understanding of connections between smoking and mortality has improved, most of them are ready now to advocate "no smoking" as part of the overall stewardship of the body. Alcohol can also have drastic personal and social effects; but with some pietistic group exceptions, most Lutherans have advocated or permitted moderate use of alcholic beverages. Surveys show Lutherans to be among the 'wettest,' so far as moderate drinking churches go, but the same surveys show less excuse or less alcoholism in Lutheran circles than one might expect where wine and liquor were not consistently frowned upon.

Q: And card-playing . . . and . . . and?

A: Card-playing never was a big deal. Maybe we have gone far enough to summarize this part. While Lutherans in practice have often admittedly been stern and strict, such practice is not of the essence of Lutheran character or faith and life. It often grew up in either hostile environments or in moments of aberration, and the like. Lutherans do not like to issue petty lists of taboos and then measure Christian life in light of them. They seek lives that are hid with Christ in God, lives that have found loving purpose, that know how to show warmth and fun and passion and love and earnestness—without always being bound by a sense of whether a practice is permitted or not. Luther himself had plenty of good times. So should his followers.

XIV.
Social and Political Attitudes

Q: We are ready then to move on to larger issues. Do Lutherans take public stands on social issues?

A: Some have, fairly recently. Many have without knowing that they did, throughout their history. Thus Lutherans usually have taken public stands in support of the nation when it is at war, not regarding that as a controversial decision or not necessarily as the only potentially God-pleasing one. Yet they have been nervous when minorities among them take stands against war or against particular wars. Some have opposed laws for abortion reform or supported laws against gambling, when these were up for debate—but rejected other kinds of Lutheran 'speaking out' on social issues. There is, obviously no clear policy or line.

Q: Maybe not, but can't you give me some guideline, some clue as to what to watch for?

A: Yes. There are some characteristics in Lutheran history. Lutherans have tended to be conservative, passive, nationalistic, authoritarian. We may not all like those adjectives, but the evidence is overwhelming about their presence in Lutheran history. Partly this results from accidents of beginnings. Luther the rebel later came to fear anarchy and came out for order. His churches took part in the rise of German and Scandinavian nationalism and enjoyed their role. Most places where they have been at all, they have been 'the establishment,' and act like one.

Q: You said that the biblical teaching was to matter so much; how does it come into play here?

A: The Bible really has two notes about God's peoples' involvements in the social and political order around them. One half is prophetic, suspicious of power, ready to 'tell off' the rulers, is subversive of the empire, casual about Herod 'that fox' and the paying of Caesar's money back to Caesar so that God could be rendered His due. The other note is supportive of order. St. Paul, for example, in inspired writings, 'wagers' that over the long haul order is better than non-order, the state better than the jungle, the bad ruler (as God's instrument) better than no rule. Lutherans have had an instinct for supporting that half.

Q: Does this attitude ever get Lutherans into trouble?

A: Yes. For one thing, it does not always go rewarded. In World War I German-American Lutherans suffered throughout the United States despite their intense loyalty, simply because America was fighting Germany overseas. For another thing, it often leads to compromise and acquiescence—as in the case of many German Lutherans who remained silent or were supportive in the rise of Hitlerism. Most often, it means that while Lutherans are loyal they are not activistic. They vote for others but do not as often run for office themselves. There has been no Lutheran president and only one Lutheran Supreme Court Justice in American history. Senators, Congressmen, Governors, and others expressive of regional interest have been in abundant supply.

Q: Is there anything distinctive about the Lutheran attitude toward the political order, then?

A: Yes; it grows out of the fundamental teaching about the Gospel. The teaching is sometimes called a 'two kingdoms' or 'two realms' theory; in it God is seen as speaking to and caring for the world in two ways. Through His commands and His law He institutes civil society for the care of the neighbor and to curb injustice. The state is not to be ruled by the Gospel or Good News of forgiveness. He speaks through that Gospel or His promises to His people in the church; it is not to be ruled by the law of God. In practice there may be some sloppiness and blurring, but the theory is emphatic.

Q: Is the civil realm, then, merely Secular?

A: Lutherans are not afraid of the idea of a secular state. They have not been in the forefront of those who seek 'Prayer Amendments' and the like. They believe that God can work out His purposes through leaders who are not of His people—as He did through Cyrus or Cornelius in the two biblical testaments. Lutherans do not wait for or work for the Christianization or Christian transforming of the state. They believe there can be 'civil righteousness' of good people who do not know God or worship Christ. Of course, they like to see Christian influence in public affairs, but their teachings do not insist on it and they know it will always be complex and compromised in that sphere.

XV. Futures

Q: In their outlook on history, are Lutherans pessimistic or optimistic?

A: Christians who work with a metaphysics of progress, in which they believe that 'behind the scenes' inside history everything can or will progress and get better, would call Christians of Lutheran persuasian pessimists. They do not look forward to such near-perfection. Cynics, fatalists, despairing people, appraising Lutheranism's desire to make a difference in the midst of a world of the demonic, the sinful, the broken, the errant, the corrupted, would call them optimists, confusing a psychological predisposition with the reality of Christian hope.

Q: What about the future? The Second Coming?

A: Lutherans believe that history will have an end; that it will be in God's hand; that He will choose the means; that His intervention in history's course will be a consummation or a fulfillment in Christ. They are informed by the many and varied biblical pictures of the future; many of these have come in the form of visions and dreams (as in the Book of Revelation at the end of the Bible), sometimes in poetry, sometimes in prophecy or pronouncement. Therefore the accounts do not always literally coincide and Lutherans are edgy about people who apply the details surely and precisely to the contemporary 'signs and wonders.' They preach this language to show that history has meaning, lives have purpose, decision is urgent, and that God will act on His promise.

Q: If they are Second Coming people, are they then millennialists?

A: No. They find millennial language, the idea of a thousand-year reign of a returned Christ, occurring only in the visionary literature and see it secondary to other accountings of future possibility. They are more at home with the language of heaven and hell, which need not be considered in spatial terms so much as in terms of a different order of being. They stand for the promise and threat that come to fulfillment in lives that receive God's gift in Christ on one hand, or on the other that permanently turn Him away, even when they turn their backs on the least of Christ's brethren. Lutherans claim to know nothing of the paving, furniture, or temperature of heaven and hell, but say only that in these pictures God has in mind realities about futures that transcend human history as we know it.

Q: What is pictured beyond death?

A: Don't hurry. Death itself is taken very seriously, as a reality that defines life and has to be reckoned with—for Christ who is risen, as well as for all believers. But death has been swallowed up in Christ's victory and its sting is gone, to use Paul's vivid imagery. Lutherans may or may not choose to speak of a subsequent immortality of the soul; many are reluctant to because the Bible says that immortality belongs only to God; because in peoples' minds immortality is seen as a natural property of all persons; because they thereby confuse Christian pictures of afterlife with Greek concepts of the soul, sprung free from the prison of the body, now rejoining undifferentiated being—whatever that is.

Q: What goes alongside of or in place of immortality, then?

A: The witness is clear: Lutherans join other Christians in their creedal affirmations of 'the resurrection of the body.' They prefer this more vital word because it does more justice to the way biblical people conceived humans: as ensouled bodies, not as embodied souls, to paraphrase one scholar. The phrase points to the unity of the human, to the reality of God's act toward each. Paul makes clear that the resurrection idea has nothing to do with resuscitation or reconstituting molecular structures ("It is sown a natural body; it is raised a spiritual body"). Resurrection points to a 'new creation,' a new kind of unimaginable reality for which biblical symbols can only serve as outlining foretastes. God's purposes for each believer are not exhausted by history or limited by death. They are enhanced, enlarged, realized, in a new realm of purpose.

Q: Mention of hell brings to mind ideas of devil and evil. What do Lutherans believe about these?

A: Unfortunately, pictures of the devil are confused by cultural expressions from medieval art to modern opera and comic strips: of a man in a red union suit, with a pitchfork tail. Lutherans consider 'the devil' to be a reality as a kind of personification of evil. (Remember that 'person' can mean more and other than it does in the human realm; thus Father, Son and Holy Spirit are 'persons,' but not as we are.) Lutherans have no special accounting for the origin of evil, nor a philosophical answer to its presence. In the cross of Jesus Christ they see God living with them the terms of existence in a world of evil, pain, suffering, and death—and conquering.

Q: You mention suffering and death; how do these fit in to the scheme of a good and loving God?

A: We do not know. In general suffering and disease are connected by the Bible with the fall of man into sin. In particular they are taught by Jesus himself not to try to connect specific diseases with specific persons, or any kind of natural disaster with special guilt. Lutherans join other Christians in praying that 'nothing shall separate them from the love of God in Christ'; they also try to discern a larger meaning in suffering; they serve those in need or in illness; they take advantage of modern means of medicine in connection with prayers for healing.

Q: Does the state, then, have the final say over huge dimensions of life?

A: Much say, yes. Final say, no. While some may be slow to assert it, in the end all Lutherans will say that 'we ought to obey God rather than men.' They may have often been nervous when appeals were made to a 'higher law' during the Civil Rights or Vietnamese dissenting cases, but they could not deny that the Bible both shows people going beyond the claims of earthly authority and commands believers to do so. Martin Niemoeller, Dietrich Bonhoeffer, Eivind Berggrav, Kaj Munk were German or Scandinavian Lutheran leaders who risked all for the sake of God's command over perversions in the state.

Q: What are Lutheran attitudes toward war?

A: From the previous description, you can gather that—however much the Lutheran population honestly hates armed conflict—Lutherans in practice have usually tended to call for loyalty and to bless the cannon. They inherited 'just war' theories, in which only victimized sides are 'just' in war, but Lutherans on both sides of battles—along with most other Christians—have almost consistently seen their side to be just. As generally conservative readers of the Bible, they know that Yahweh's people were often involved in sanctioned wars. So they have made less of the New Testament and especially Jesus in their attitude toward violence. In recent years, this picture is growing more complex and there is more Lutheran dissent.

Q: Can Lutherans be pacifists?

A: Probably, yes; pacifism is one way of reading the Sermon on the Mount or working out a philosophy of obeying God, the giver of life, rather than fallen, greedy, murderous man who takes life. But few Lutherans have been consistent convinced total pacifists on models of the Quakers, the Mennonites, and the Church of the Brethren. From Martin Luther down through American Lutheran denominations during the Vietnamese War, however, there have been calls and allowances for what has come to be called 'selective conscientious objection.' Luther says that the person who kills in a war that he knows and regards to be unjust is committing murder.

Q: A corollary question, then? what about capital punishment?

A: No surprises here: given that 'hawkish' sounding attitude toward war, one might expect that Lutherans have not very consistently opposed capital punishment. They live up to that expectation. In our times, both on humanitarian grounds, because capital punishment has not been shown to be a deterrent—and because of emerging concepts of rehabilitation or the value and potential of life—more and more Lutherans oppose capital punishment. There has been no consistent official position, but because the Bible permits it or gives illustrations of it, more Lutherans than not have accepted or called for the practice.

Q: Are Lutherans in America 'separationists' on matters of church and state?

A: Given their 'two realms' theory, they would be predisposed toward policies advocating separation of church and state. And most of them go along with what they think is the American policy. Yet they tend not to be strict or wholly consistent. They accept tax exemption for church property—which is an indirect state subsidy. All but one small Lutheran group provide military and institutional chaplains in the pay of the state. Few oppose governmental funds for non-religious buildings on denominational college campuses; not all have turned their backs on some forms of support of their parochial schools. But despite all this, they tend more toward separation than toward blurring and converging.

Q: How does the Lutheran try to make an impact in society and serve God there?

A: Lutherans are not inhumane, they do not turn their backs on injustice or poverty or racial hatred—though their overall record may be as bad as most other Christians! They may occasionally 'make pronouncements' as denominations or through interest groups, but they realize the limits both of these and of public demonstrations. Sometimes they may take a minor part in working for legislation —especially when issues directly concerning the church come up. But they tend to believe that they should prepare forgiven people to be free citizens, working for good in the commonwealth without always speaking explicitly for the churches.

XVI.
Summing Up

Q: Do Lutherans consider theirs to be the only true grasp of the Gospel?

A: Yes. But they do not think they are the only ones who grasp it thus. I threw this one in to remind myself of a similar answer to a similar question some years ago by the late editor, G. Elson Ruff. He went on to point out that if they believed other Gospels to be true, Lutherans would form a different Church or find one. But they do not think that only Lutherans properly understand the Gospel. They do not talk much about 'the invisible Church'—an essentially Calvinistic term in Protestantism—but they regard the borders of the Church to be invisible or at least blurred, and do not want to be arrogant about their 'monopoly' on truth.

Q: Has Lutheranism any congenital faults?

A: Yes. In this book we have not tried to hide Lutheranism's weak points, to do a public relations 'puff' job. In summary, we can say that Lutherans have often been stand-offish, arrogant, condescending toward other Christians in their defense of the truth of the Gospel as they saw it. They have often been passive in the social realm, relegating to other Christians the responsibility of serving people whose needs or experienced injustices result not from individual sin so much as from societal structural flaws. Other faults—heedlessness in the face of need, half-heartedness and lukewarmness, and the like, are shared with Christians who come at elements of the faith in different ways and are not special problems for Lutherans as Lutherans.

Q: Is Lutheranism a force for good in the world?

A: Yes, whenever and insofar as and to the extent that it proclaims, realizes, and embodies the reality of God's grace and favor in the event of Jesus Christ; whenever it opens the scriptural word of freedom and liberation and turns it loose among people, whenever it makes 'faith active in love,' whenever it breathes through the Holy Spirit the spirit of hope in a despairing world. Lutheranism is a force for good whenever it does any of these things. And it often does.

The Author

Martin E. Marty is the Fairfax M. Cone Distinguished Service Professor of the history of modern Christianity at The University of Chicago. He is senior editor of **The Christian Century** weekly, editor of the fortnightly **Context**, and coeditor of the quarterly **Church History**. He has been president of the American Academy of Religion, the American Society of Church History, the American Catholic Historical Association, and the Park Ridge Center for the Study of Health, Faith, and Ethics. He won the National Book Award for **Righteous Empire**, one of his forty or more books. He has written on **Lutheranism** for **Encyclopedia Britannica**. Ordained in 1952, he is an active Lutheran minister and member of Ascension Lutheran Church, Riverside, Illinois.